W9-AIA-479

RETURN TO
Hospice Volunteer Services
P.O. Box 772
Middlebury, VT 05753
802-388-4111

living with an empty chair

living with an empty chair:
a guide through grief
enlarged edition

by Dr. Roberta Temes
Downstate Medical Center

✳ IRVINGTON PUBLISHERS, INC.
NEW HORIZON PRESS PUBLISHERS
NEW YORK

Copyright 1984 by Irvington Publishers, Inc.

First Irvington Edition 1980

Copyright 1977 by Mandala

All rights reserved. No part of this book may be reproduced in any manner whatever, including information storage or retrieval, in whole or in part (except for brief quotations in critical articles or reviews), without written permission from the publisher. For information, write to Irvington Publishers, Inc., 551 Fifth Avenue, New York, New York 10017.

Library of Congress Cataloging in Publication Data

Temes, Roberta.
　Living with an empty chair.

　Bibliography: p.
　1. Grief.　2. Bereavement—Psychological aspects.
I. Title.
BF575.G7T45　1984　　　155.9'37　　　83-12894
ISBN 0-8290-1473-X
ISBN 0-88282-002-8 (New Horizon)

Photo credits: p. 58, R. Burdich/Leo de Wys; pp. 61, 69, 72, E. Johnson/Leo de Wys; p. 63, Kontaxis/Leo de Wys; p. 66, R. Weldon/Leo de Wys; p. 75, C. Hulstein/Leo de Wys; p. 80, Leo de Wys; p. 94, R. Laird/Leo de Wys
All other photographs by Audrey Konicek
Drawings and design by Amy Maid
Typography by Dimensional Graphics, Roselle, New Jersey

Printed in the United States of America

table of contents

Dedicated to my mother
Eleanor "Nan" Rempell
A wise and wonderful woman.

introduction

Books with information about death, about the psychological experiences of the dying person, and even about life after death, are on today's best-seller list. *Living With An Empty Chair — A Guide Through Grief* is not of that genre. Instead, this book addresses those of you who are not dying; you who must continue living, even though someone you love is dead.

Within these pages you will find a combination of psychological and practical advice. You will learn about the bereavement process and be guided through the stages of grief.

If you are recently bereaved you will utilize this information in order to understand precisely what is happening to you.

If you are a psychotherapist, psychologist, or social worker, you will use what you read in order to better help your client.

If you are a physician or nurse, please share this book with your bereaved patient to contribute to the process of healing.

If you are a funeral director or monument builder you will gain sensitivity to the needs of the families you serve by reading this book.

If you are a student of psychology, social work, or education you will increase your fund of knowledge by studying this as a text.

If you are a concerned neighbor, friend, or family member of a bereaved person please offer this book as a gift of comfort.

There is a comprehensive, annotated bibliography suggesting books and articles for both the layperson and the professional at the end of the book.

Since most bereaved people are females (widows now outnumber widowers more than 5 to 1), and since choice of pronoun is the author's prerogative, the word "she" is used throughout this work to designate a person of unknown gender.

Notice that bereavement, mourning, and grief are used interchangeably rather than according to their strictest definitions.

Please understand that there are no outside authorities on death or bereavement. We each experience the death of someone we love in our own unique style. Your experience is valid for you and your response is right for you. If you are bereaved, you are hurting. This book will not take away the hurt. It will, though, explain the whys and wherefores of your pain; sometimes anxiety is allayed when a feeling or experience is labeled.

Living With An Empty Chair — A Guide Through Grief is based upon the assumption that although there is now an empty chair in your house, your thoughts and feelings are still very much attached to the person who occupied that chair. The relationship still exists.

1

death as a normal life crisis

Death is a fact of life.

It has, of course, always been so. Yet only now, in the final quarter of the Twentieth Century, is death being acknowledged as worthy of open, investigative discussion. Death is now where sex was twenty years ago — just coming out of the closet. Anthropologist Margaret Mead has written that "when a person is born we rejoice, and when they're married we jubilate, but when they die we try to pretend nothing has happened."

In our society there is no formalized way to sever the relationship you have maintained with the deceased. What are you to do with the emotional investment of a lifetime? The body may be buried, but the emotions of those who love the deceased continue to survive.

LIFE CRISES

Death is a normal life crisis. Other normal life crises include marriage, the birth of off-spring, and divorce. Engagement helps us adapt to our new role as marriage partner; pregnancy permits us nine months to prepare for parenthood; and separation prepares us for divorce. Moving to a new neighborhood is a normal life crisis and usually some version of the "Welcome Wagon" is present to help us cope and adjust. Leaving one job and accepting a new one also is a crisis. We are expected to be anxious about beginning the new. This is normal.

Institutionalized preparation periods notwithstanding, we still anticipate difficult emotional reactions during these normal life crises. Each bride, mother, and divorcee, if she feels unsure or flounders in her new position, is reassured that she is simply experiencing a "period of adjustment."

With the loss of someone close to you, you are also going through a normal life crisis. You, too, need a period of adjustment. How do you deal with the powerful emotions that threaten to overwhelm you? It is likely that you have no guide to follow during that painful period after the death of a loved one. You have no preparation for your new role as mourner. Please be assured that while the physical presence of the person has been eliminated, *the relationship still exists*.

Grief is not a disease. There is no magic pill to achieve a quick cure. Grief is a long, agonizing process, but it does have an end. Grief is usually experienced in three distinct stages. Each stage must be gone through in its entirety before you can feel "back to normal." Experiencing the pain of grief at the appropriate point in time prevents the deeper pain of delayed grief. Thus, advice such as "keep a stiff upper lip" or "snap out of it; there's so much to live for," however well-meaning, is potentially harmful. The griever can simply thank the well-wisher, and proceed through her journey of grief.

EFFECTS OF POSTPONING GRIEF

The effects of unresolved grief can be serious. Some bereaved individuals find it too painful to mourn. They postpone a confrontation with their feelings for as long as is possible. They fill every hour of day and evening with frantic activity. Then months, or even years later, a seemingly insignificant loss will set off an inappropriate grief reaction. The person can panic and not understand what is happening. The answer, of course, is that the mourning process is just beginning.

DENIAL OF GRIEF

The absence of mourning symptoms is a warning signal. Denial is an unconscious psychological defense. Everyone uses some denial during the course of a life time. Children and psychotics use it often. When there is a thought, a wish, or a fact that is intolerable for you to confront, the denial process intervenes and separates you from the pain. Denial acts like an aspirin: the ache is still there, but you do not experience it. When you use denial, danger is not overwhelming, reality is not painful.

If you find that you are behaving as if nothing has happened and have no outward signs of mourning, or if you are behaving as if something wonderful has happened and you are euphoric most of the time, it would be worthwhile to visit a psychotherapist or other qualified bereavement counselor.

Some people feel they must always be strong and in control. If you are this way, please understand that in this situation *it is a sign of strength to be able to express* your emotions. It is absolutely essential that your feelings be released. If they are not released through words and tears, they will find expression through other ways. Sometimes serious illnesses occur when the bereaved is unable to express her feelings.

PSYCHOLOGY OF GRIEF

Freud defined mourning as a "conscious reaction to the loss of a loved one." Psychoanalysts today usually say that mourning consists of a conventional ritual determined by the particular social, cultural, and religious groups to which you belong. Grief is the term usually used to describe the psychological and physiological reactions you are experiencing: that is, those things that are happening now in your mind and in your body.

Bereavement is a psychologically necessary state. Even though you feel terrible, *it is healthy for you to be feeling that way now*. As you proceed through the stages of bereavement you will become increasingly liberated from the agony of your recent experience with death. Ultimately, the dual goals of the mourning process will be realized. These two goals, signifying the end of bereavement, are (1) to complete the emotional relationship with the deceased and (2) to refocus your life's energies toward the future.

In psychoanalytic terms we are discussing the process of de-cathexis. When we place much emotion and value onto someone, that person becomes cathected (emotionally valued) for us. To gradually displace some of that emotion onto other people and things is called de-cathexis. This is a long process. You cannot finish bereavement quickly, but you *can* finish it.

2

STAGES OF GRIEF

Have you begun the bereavement process yet?

There are predictable stages of the bereavement process. Not everyone experiences the same feelings at the same points in time, but grief does typically include three distinct stages. These stages may be called numbness, disorganization, and reorganization.

NUMBNESS

The first stage of bereavement begins at the moment of death, and continues for the next several weeks or months. If you are fortunate, during this time your family, friends and neighbors are concerned and solicitous. They are there to be leaned upon, physically and psychologically. You may be surprised to notice yourself maintaining an emotional distance from these helpers. That is because you are not yet ready to deal with all your powerful feelings. You must perform certain tasks, such as funeral arrangements or estate settlements, which require your immediate attention. Your field of vision is restricted to the accomplishment and discharge of these current chores. Your functioning may be automatic, mechanical and robot-like. That is because you are still numb from the shock of the death. You may feel as if you are suspended in an unreal state. During this initial stage of grief you may be unable to grasp the full significance of your loss. You may feel as if you are involved in a bad dream which will soon be over. This is your mind's way of protecting you from fully recognizing the painful finality of death.

One emotion which occasionally surfaces at this early stage, aside from genuine sorrow, is a fleeting feeling of anger toward the deceased. Immediately guilt takes over and neutralizes that anger, which may emerge during the next phase of the grief process.

DISORGANIZATION

A second or middle phase of grief begins as soon as the insulation provided by shock starts to wear off. Several weeks or months have passed since the death. The haze is lifting. Friends and family have resumed their former commitments, and are not as attentive as they have been. Your neighbor, who each day checked in to see how you were doing, now comes by only once a week. The relatives who telephoned long distance now just write occasionally. The children who came home from school, or traveled from their homes across the continent, now are immersed in their regular routines. It seems that, for everyone else, life has returned to what it was before the death. It is ironic, and sad, that now, when you can finally appreciate intimacy and no longer want, or need, to feel distant from others, there are few with whom to share your feelings. The numbness lifts, and the full meaning of the loss is felt. You actually feel a vacuum. There is acute loneliness and emptiness where there was once life. These are *normal* and *appropriate* feelings during this stage of bereavement.

Friends and relatives may become alarmed. ("She was taking it so well, but now look at her. She must be having a nervous breakdown.") Those friends and relatives do not realize that a disorganization of personality, including symptoms of depression, are to be expected now. Aimlessness and apathy, loss of appetite and loss of sleep, constant weeping, are all indications of the pain and the despair you feel. Universal symptoms of grief include feelings of tightness in your throat, shortness of breath, the need to frequently sigh, and extreme fatigue.

YEARNING

Perhaps you are feeling restless and cannot concentrate. If so, it may be that you have not yet fully accepted your loss as permanent. Your constant search for "something to interest me" may be a disguised way of searching for your loved one. Your urge to recover your lost one, your yearning and your hope, create feelings of anxiety and panic. Gradually, as reality intrudes, you will give up hoping for that reunion and begin accepting and adjusting. This may not make you feel better, though. While the anxiety you felt was a reaction to the danger of a loss, the increasing awareness of the loss brings pain.

During this phase you are feeling a persistent pain of loneliness and at the same time are being confronted with new responsibilities. Whether it is winterizing the car, taking out the garbage, or diapering the baby, you are performing chores that were once someone else's obligation. Each of these is now a reminder that "someone else" is dead.

TRANSITIONAL OBJECTS

Objects belonging to the deceased may take on particular emotional significance. When you were a toddler and had to be separated from your mother, you probably had a comforting reminder of her to carry around during her absence. Such reminders are called transitional objects by the professionals, but are more familiarly known as security blankets.

Perhaps you are using a transitional object now, to remind you of your lost loved one. Most people do need some articles of the deceased which they sometimes sleep with, wear, hold, or simply look at. This is normal behavior.

The layer of psychological protection developed during the initial stage of grief has diminished and as you experience the pain of deep feelings you may be resentful and feel sorry for yourself. Again, *this is normal*. Sorrow for self is a fundamental part of grief work. It is necessary for you to feel sorry for yourself and for your predicament.

ANGER

Other emotions yearning for expression during the middle phase of mourning are shame, fear, guilt, hopelessness and helplessness, and anger. Feelings of anger that were brief during the initial stage are likely now to reoccur with greater frequency and strength. Your anger should not be stifled by those attempting to help you. Even rage is appropriate at this point. William Shakespeare gives recognition to the bereaved's anger in a passage in King Henry the VI:

"We mourn in black: why mourn we not in blood?"

To hide from the anger you feel toward the deceased is to risk developing symptoms at a later date, symptoms which may be far more difficult to deal with than the original anger.

In "The Angry Book," psychiatrist Theodore Rubin describes a patient as follows:

I remember a woman I had in treatment who suffered from a very severe, ugly lesion that covered most of her body . . . She had been to many doctors to no avail . . . Marcy was an extremely self-effacing, compliant woman who spent most of her early treatment hours in an effort to convince me of how really happy she was. She told me that she adored her dead father as well as her gentle, sweet, devoted mother (still alive). Her image of herself was very much like her image of her mother. She did not remember ever having been angry. The reason for her refusal to see a psychoanalyst soon became apparent. She simply did not wish to disturb a just-too-perfect image. And disturbed it became! After months of work — particularly of analysis of dreams — it became apparent that she did in fact love her father but was also happy that he died.

These seemingly mutually exclusive emotional entities are extremely common in human psychology. Marcy felt that her father's death was revenge and a vindictive triumph over her mother. As time went on, the twisting of this rage became unnecessary. Strengthened by our relationship she became aware that her anger did not kill her father nor did anger make her an evil person. For two years she did little else than report to me three times a week and sound off enormous anger — and as she did so, her skin cleared. Eventually the lesion disappeared and was replaced by healthy tissue. Much subsequent work relieved her of the need to be sweet and angelic (with an enraged skin). She chose instead just to be human.

This is an extreme case, but the message to you is clear. You are indeed angry. You have been abandoned by someone you love. You have a right to ask, "Why me?" Your feelings of anger are proof that you are human. Many people in your circumstance are embarrassed to notice that they are hostile in the presence of those very people who are trying to help. This often occurs; soon your hostility will disappear. Meanwhile, while it is part of you, neither harbor it nor deny it; be it.

GUILT

Do you feel guilty because the death has brought you some relief? It is perfectly appropriate to feel relieved at the same time that you are feeling devastated. You should be allowed to ventilate these feelings.

If your loss occurred at the end of a long illness, then even though you miss the person, a part of you may be relieved because your physical responsibilities have ended. The task of caring for a dying person can be dreadfully difficult.

The difficulty is compounded if the fatal illness was a secret (either *from* the dying person or *between* you and the dying person). Keeping a secret from someone you love meant that all interaction with that person had some duplicity. You were always under a strain and had no way to express your feelings. You now may feel relieved from carrying that burden of deception.

Close meaningful relationships permit the luxury of shouting, yelling, feeling resentful, maybe even saying "Drop dead" or "I hope you never return." While normal human beings are capable of anger, they are not endowed with magical powers. Anger cannot kill. Guilt feelings must somehow now be *expressed* in order for you to experience that which you already know on an intellectual level — that the death did not occur because of your wish or your words. Unresolved guilt is a basic problem of bereavement.

AMBIVALENCE

Whatever loss you feel is valid, regardless of the superficial quality of the relationship. Even the occasional harsh words you had with the deceased are proof of the intimacy you shared. We do not argue with strangers. We care enough to pursue an issue only with people whose opinions we value. The husband who fought furiously with his wife is in the same pain, and going through the same grief, as the husband who showed only kindness toward his wife. The daughter grieving for the mother with whom she had daily shouting matches is suffering as much as the compliant daughter who never disagreed with her parent. When intense feelings are invested there is always a deep and complicated emotional relationship.

Acknowledging the negative as well as the positive traits of the deceased will help you proceed through grief at a steady pace. Setbacks in the process occur when you are unable to recognize those parts of the deceased person's personality which were disagreeable to you. This is not easy. It is difficult to endure the expression of painful emotions. In fact, the passage through the stages of bereavement is work. It is called grief work. Grief work is the emotional reorganization you must attend to before life can return to normal. Grief work is hard work. That may be why you are so often tired.

BEHAVING BY HABIT

During this middle phase of mourning, you may "forget" that the person you loved is permanently gone. This is *normal* and should not be interpreted as "sick" behavior. Rather, it is behavior propelled by habit. A new widow who, for forty years, has set a dinner table for two, may continue to do so. The widower, upon hearing the phone ring, may automatically request his wife to "please get the phone, hon."

Be assured. It is normal to occasionally act as if the dead person is still alive. Bereaved people sometimes hallucinate during this stage. The wife so desperately wishes to hear the familiar sounds indicating that her husband has returned from a day's work that she is certain she hears the car pulling into the driveway, or his key turning in the lock. Similarly the widower may insist that he can smell his wife's perfume, or hear her footsteps. Bereaved parents frequently report that they hear their child crying. A college student reported that she once ran completely across campus, pursuing a young woman whom she thought was her recently deceased sister. Many bereaved people look forward to dreams that permit them to interact, once again, with the deceased. Reports of ghosts, haunted houses, and footsteps in the night, as well as some reports of successful seances, may be attributed to the urgent wish to be in contact with the deceased.

The hallucination gives a sense of presence and helps maintain the feeling that your loved one is nearby.

REVIEWING YOUR RELATIONSHIP

Just as you now have a need to talk about your feelings, you may also have a need to talk about both the life and the death of your loved one. As you proceed through this troublesome time it becomes psychologically necessary to review the details of the life you shared with the deceased. Whether or not your listeners consider it a tedious review, it is important that you are encouraged to speak of the past. You may wish to inform your friends or family that this need will not persist indefinitely.

Soon you will go on to other things — such as speaking about all aspects of the actual death. It may be necessary for you to reiterate every last detail. Often people spend weeks telling friends exactly what they ate for breakfast on that fateful day. Such recounting should be encouraged.

You must be permitted to freely speak about the circumstances of the death. In order to incorporate the finality of the situation you will need to re-live those last few days or hours. Professor Philip Pecorino, of City University, New York, has termed this process "psychic slapping." Over and over you bombard your mind with the details of the death, until finally you recognize the reality of the situation. Again, apprise your friends: this is something you need to do *now*, not forever.

ACTING CRAZY

Symptoms of the middle phase of mourning closely resemble some symptoms of mental illness. The difference, of course, is that indications of mental illness do not spontaneously and permanently disappear, while indications of grief will eradicate themselves as the mourning process is completed.

The distinguished actress, Helen Hayes, when asked to comment on her adjustment to widowhood, candidly admitted: "For two years I was just as crazy as you can be and still be at large. It was total confusion. How did I come out of it? I don't know, because I didn't know when I was in it that I was in it."

Lynn Caine substantiates this in her autobiographical book "Widow." She writes, "During my crazy periods I made terrible financial mistakes. And that's why I keep repeating my advice to widows. Sit. Be quiet. Don't move. You have to understand that your mind is not working properly, even though you think it is. Protect yourself from yourself."

Ms. Caine describes her inability to be at peace with herself during the mid-phase of mourning. "I had to do something. That, of course, is the trap most widows fall into. The most difficult advice in the world to follow is "Do Nothing."

In an effort to be helpful to you, some well-wishers may respond to your grief symptoms as if they were symptoms of severe mental illness. It is important for you to know and remind yourself: *if you were not mentally ill prior to the death of your loved one, you will recover from bereavement and regain your ability to function.* Bereavement happens to an existing personality. You have strengths, weaknesses, and previous experiences of coping with loss. To cope is to acknowledge that a problem exists and then to decide upon a course of action. The combination of your personality structure and the expertise of the helpers available to you can often determine how rocky or smooth the road through bereavement will be.

Recovery from grief is enhanced and hastened if you are able to experience the temporary, but necessary, irrational feelings and thoughts which are normal during mourning. If you allow yourself to feel all your feelings, and if you can develop a total acceptance of your brief period of craziness, you will soon be well again. Pause for a moment. How are you feeling? What are you feeling? Are your grief responses similar to those described here? How are they different? Remember, you are a distinct and unique personality. Learn to become aware of your feelings. Then *trust* those feelings.

REORGANIZATION

Middle-phase mourners find the complexity of life threatening and frightening. The daily tasks of living seem overwhelming. But as you emerge through the mid-phase of grief, you again find the world secure and rewarding.

The dual task of mourning, completion of the emotional relationship with the deceased, and re-directing of energy toward the future, usually begins to be accomplished somewhere between the first and second anniversary of the death. Gradually you weep less and have less of a need to indiscriminately talk about the deceased. Sleep and appetite are being restored. You may be surprised to find that occasionally several hours, and perhaps a full day, might pass during which your mind does not automatically return to thoughts of the deceased. Upon awakening, the first thought of the day is sometimes not of the deceased, but of the day's activities. This end phase of mourning is a relief. Life is no longer one frantic anxiety attack. There is a commitment to the future: you know that the dead person will never be forgotten, but you also know that your life will continue.

If you are lucky, there is someone in your environment who will acknowledge any gestures which signify a willingness to re-enter a full life. A hesitant phone call, an inquiry about a future meeting or event, a tentative plan — all these should be encouraged by the helping friend or relative. The helper has definite tasks to perform during each stage of grief. During stage one of the mourning process, the helper is there to be leaned upon and give concrete assistance with managing necessary chores. During stage two the helper must provide sanction to ventilate emotions, all emotions, and must tirelessly listen to the repeated stories about the life and death of the loved one. Now, in the last stage of mourning, the helper must be there to help expand a social network and encourage involvement and interest in life.

You have successfully completed mourning. You understand that the world has been impoverished because of this death, but you, personally, have not been impoverished. You are, once again, whole. You care, once again, about yourself. You are re-organizing your life toward the future. You are calm, but you may still have terrible days. As time passes such days will occur with less frequency.

Try not to be alarmed by occasional setbacks. Some people find that they may do well for an entire year only to find themselves virtually incapacitated by grief during the days surrounding the anniversary of the death. Such anniversary reactions are normal. In fact, Judaic law has a prescribed ritual for "death days" — the anniversary of the death. You are expected to need to discharge extra emotions during those days. The deceased will never be forgotten but the relationship is in its proper perspective. Your grief work is finishing. The pleasures of living now have more appeal than the thought of joining the deceased in death. A new stage of life is about to begin.

Stages of Grief	DURATION	CHARACTERISTICS
Stage One: NUMBNESS	Several weeks or months	Mechanical functioning Insulation
Stage Two: DISORGANIZATION	Many months	Painful feelings: loneliness depression weeping. Sleep and appetite difficulties. Sorrow for self, hallucinations.
Stage Three: REORGANIZATION	Several weeks or months	Occasional peacefulness. Less intensity of feelings.

NEEDS	DEVELOPMENTAL TASK	HELPER FUNCTIONS
Emotional distance.	To protect self from feeling impact of loss.	Assist with chores.
Intimacy, ventilation of feelings.	Acknowledge impact of loss.	Permit expression of *all* feelings. Listen to talk about life together and details of death.
Encouragement to re-enter life's mainstream.	Complete emotional relationship with deceased.	Expand social network.

3

children and grief

Responsible parents prepare their children for life's crises.

Parents read books to the child who is about to have a tonsillectomy, preparing her for that event. Prior to a first venture away from home, parents help their child anticipate feelings of homesickness. Nowadays, parents speak realistically with their children about formerly taboo subjects. They discuss future responsibilities, sex, religious ideologies, and methods of child rearing. When it comes to death, the one crisis all children will confront, parents become mute. Death education has not yet been incorporated into the family agenda. Parents prefer pretending that they will live forever.

It is, of course, the parents' own uncomfortableness with the subject that prohibits family discussion. The parent wants to protect the child from hurt and sadness, yet the denial inherent in such "rescuing" actually is a disservice. For instance, if the parent rushes to the pet store to replace the dead goldfish that has just been flushed away, that parent denies the child an opportunity to understand and accept death. The child should be able to come home from school and *see* a dead pet. She will then learn that she can face death, can mourn, and can eventually overcome grief.

When children have the opportunity to deal with the death of someone upon whom they were not dependent, their chances of successfully coping with subsequent deaths is enhanced.

All children are *always* sensitive to their parents' unstated feelings, their hidden agendas. Children become confused when parents are confused. They feel uneasy when parents give them incomplete or incorrect information. A child knows when the truth has been distorted or withheld. Such deception, while intended to help, actually harms.

Recognizing that adults are apprehensive talking about death, children, for whom the world is bewildering under the best of circumstances, can have serious difficulty comprehending death.

As soon as a parent can accept the death, and all the emotions that the death engenders, the child will begin to feel more comfortable.

EXPRESSING FEELINGS

Children and adolescents have the capacity to write about their experiences with death; the young adult especially has the ability to put thoughts and feelings into words. It is a helpful way to express emotions and continue working through the mourning process, and parents should encourage it.

Below, an adolescent boy describes his reaction to a death that occurred during his early childhood:

> "When I was six years old my grandfather died of cancer. We found out that he had cancer about six months before his death. It had spread too far for treatment to do any good. The doctor would come once a week to bring him medicine for the pain.
>
> On the day he died my mother was doing some work in the garden. It was a sunny day, toward the end of June. I was sitting in his room talking to him. He told me that he was leaving to go with my grandmother, who died four years earlier. He kissed me good-bye and told me to tell my brother good-bye. Then he asked me to tell him a story of one of the books my mother had read to me. When I finished the story he had died. I went outside and told my mother that something was wrong because "soap suds" were coming out of his mouth. When she came in she started to scream and cry. She insisted I go to a neighbor's house for the rest of the day. I couldn't understand why she reacted this way. My grandfather seemed content, so I thought that we should be happy too."

Third graders at Public School 195 in Brooklyn, New York, spontaneously responded with compassion and sincerity when informed that their teacher was absent because of the death of her husband. Some students demonstrated a maturity which could be gained only by having gone though a difficult life experience themselves.

"Dear Mrs. Gingold,

I know your sad. you suffered a very big loss. I am very sorry for you.
The same thing happend to me. My mother is getting married after the summer.

Love,
Bruce"

"Dear Mrs. Gingold,

I did not expect you to cheer up. It will stay with you for the rest of your life.

Love,
Georgie "

Others accepted their teacher's inevitable feelings of sadness and acknowledged that although they wish she would "cheer up" she needed to be sad at this time in her life.

"Dear Mrs. Gingold,

I'm sorry your husband died. He was a nice man. I would feel the same way you would.

Sincerely yours,

Kimberly"

"Dear Mrs. Gingold,

I know what sadness has come to you. I'm sorry about it too!
I wish you would cheer up, but I know how you feel.

Sincerely,

Patti"

Some of the students intuitively felt that their teacher would be needing an external motivation in order to re-enter life, and offered her evidence of their love and of their need for her.

"Dear Mrs. Gingold,

I miss you so much that I'm mad. I feel sorry
for your loss. I know that you feel sad but maybe
we can all help you to feel better soon. Come
back as soon as you can.

Love,

Rachel"

"Dear Mrs. Gingold,

I hope you be happy soon.
I feeling sad because your sad.
I'm sorry this happened to you and I hope
you won't cry no more. We will all help you.
And we will always love you. We all miss you.

Love,

Josephine"

Some students lamented the inevitability of death.

"Dear Mrs. Gingold,

We are all very sorry for what happened to your
husband. We know how sad you are and we feel the
same way about it. We all wish that it didn't happen
but that is nature.
Love, Ilana, Ari, Jella, Vera, and Sasha"

Another student philosophically wrote about the anticipated birth of a grandchild.

"Dear Mrs. Gingold,

*I am very sorry for what happened to your
husband. I hope you'll feel better when your daughter has a baby.*

    Sincerely yours,

    Avery"

Like children everywhere, all of Mrs. Gingold's students knew exactly how they were feeling and were able to clearly convey their message. Children can be trusted to respond with innate wisdom, once they have been told the truth. Had Mrs. Gingold's husband been a member of their immediate family, some facts of the death may have been withheld in an effort to shield them; and therein would begin a breeding ground for future doubts and difficulties.

CHILDRENS' GRIEF REACTIONS

The grief of a child for a parent or sibling is particularly painful. To a child, death may be taken as the ultimate rejection. In childish magical thinking, death occurs because of a deed or a wish. Some children, convinced that they caused the death, feel guilty for the remainder of their lives.

For the child to properly grow emotionally after the death of a parent, she must first want to continue living. She must be assured that although she might even like to join the beloved parent in death, life itself, including its current pain, does have some special joys to offer her. Children do not usually feel depressed on a conscious level, but a perceptive observer might note an increasingly apathetic attitude. A child's enthusiasm and motivation may die in an unconscious effort to be dead like her parent. If a child is assured of future care she is less likely to be tempted to want to join her parent in death.

While most adults begin the first stage of mourning immediately, children usually begin mourning several weeks or months after the death. Children should not be criticized for caring, selfishly, about their own personal needs at the time of parental death. The child who asks "But who will take me to the ball game?" or "Who'll braid my hair for me each morning?" or "What's for dinner?" when everyone else is weeping, is not being unduly selfish. She is responding as a child should respond.

Children often assume a different pattern of grief than adults, because their dependent status is felt more. They sometimes postpone mourning until they are assured that all their needs for survival will be taken care of. Once they are positive that their physical and psychological security will not be snatched from them, they will relax and feel, and weep, and begin the mourning process.

Children need this initial period of time to test their environment and guarantee their future care. It is not easy for a youngster to mourn. She has spent much of her life learning how to gain control of her impulses. Previous experiences have challenged her ability *not* to "let go and cry." Now she needs plenty of time to gain courage and become brave enough to risk feeling the depth of the loss.

A DUAL TASK FOR THE PARENT

The surviving parent has the overwhelming responsibility of dealing with her own grief and getting her own life back in order, and of helping the child proceed through the mourning process. It is not easy and the parent needs all the help she can get. *The child gets permission to mourn from the surviving parent.* To prevent the child from remaining in an acute anxiety state, and to help the child begin to mourn, the parent *should try to continue the daily routine* and not change the child's environment. This is not the time for a new house, a new school or even a new baby-sitter.

The parent should look for cues indicating the child's readiness to grieve. From that point on they should weep together, pray together, reminisce together, and especially talk together. Talk is necessary because children are full of misconceptions.

CLEARING UP MISCONCEPTIONS

Children need to talk in order to clarify. They must be told that the person is dead. Other "stories" do not work. To say that the deceased is on a long trip is only to create future problems regarding traveling and separating. To say that the deceased is in a deep sleep is to create future bedtime difficulties. The child must be told that death is final. When parents do not use the term 'dead' they encourage hope. Only when she knows that there is absolutely no hope of the deceased returning, will the child start to accept the finality of the situation and permit herself to grieve. There is, thus, an advantage for children to witness the actual burial. Cremations and other forms of body disposal do not seem to help the mourner as much as does an earth burial.

The following account illustrates the kind of confusion and ambiguity that can result from a parent using a euphemism for the verb "to die."

> *"At age 3 or 4 while shopping with my mother, I overheard a conversation with a neighbor — 'It's a shame she lost her mother — she was so young.' I envisioned a girl my age walking out of a store, noticing her mother wasn't following, and not being able to find her. I asked my mother if the girl had found her mother. I don't remember her answer but it could not have been very meaningful because for years I couldn't understand why the girl had stopped looking for her mother, and how it was possible for them to never find each other."*

If you plan to explain the concept of heaven to a child you must carefully choose your words. Children calmly take things literally. Stewardesses report that each plane to Disneyland has at least one child peering out the window trying to locate the grandma who died. Children have been known to ask, "If brother went to heaven, why are you burying him in the earth?" One young child thought that bodies were 'planted' in the ground so that new ones would grow.

Rabbi Earl Grollman, in one of his several very helpful books about death, recounts that in the movie "Yours, Mine and Ours" there is a scene in which Lucille Ball, as a young widow, reprimands her son for misbehaving. He responds by saying "I'm being naughty because you said God takes those who are good, and I don't want God to take me."

Attitudes that affect the child of a deceased parent may be the result of unconscious assumptions. If mourning is not properly completed, the child may feel, on an unconscious level, that if she dares to love again, the object of her love will again be taken away from her. She may never risk developing a close relationship for the rest of her life. This is extreme, of course, but it certainly occurs.

Children should not be told that they are now "the man, (or woman) of the house." In spite of some reshuffling of personal duties in the household, the child's childhood still belongs to her. Children need to be able to act in their childish, dependent ways in order to get the care and the cuddling they deserve.

It is important for the surviving parent to discuss with the child ways in which the child and the deceased are similar and also different. Children have a desire to identify with their parent who is dead, but are often afraid that if they have some of their deceased relative's characteristics, they too may die. The sensitive surviving parent seeks to enhance the child's identification with the deceased parent's traits where appropriate, and point out differences from the deceased where appropriate. Bereaved children, like some bereaved adults, sometimes believe they have the same symptoms that caused their parent's death. It is necessary to talk to the child about the disease and about the possibility of developing similar symptoms but not the same disease. Children may need to be shown evidence that illness does not necessarily lead to death. We all get sick and we all recover; health is a natural state. It is the rare exception who succumbs to disease.

FUNERALS AND MEMORIALS

So vital is adult support and presence during commemorative services that a child's attendance at the funeral will be a good experience for her only if a familiar adult accompanies her and holds her hand, literally, throughout. If the adult is someone the child knows and trusts, she will not be overwhelmed by the proceedings. Before the funeral begins, the person chosen to be with the child should explain in detail what will happen during the ceremonies. The child should be informed about the casket and decide ahead of time whether or not she wishes to see the body, if in fact the casket is open. After the child is told all about the services (and prepared for the possibility of adults weeping and perhaps becoming hysterical) she may choose not to attend the funeral. That is her prerogative.

A young mother wrote the following account of her daughter's first encounter with death and with a funeral home:

> "My daughter lost her great grandmother when she was three. I made arrangements with the funeral director to bring my daughter to the funeral home before it was open — so she could see her grandmother and we could talk privately without family and friends present. The funeral director let us in and then disappeared. I must stop to describe the room Grandma was laid out in. Although I hadn't really noticed it, I realized later how awesome it must have appeared to my daughter.
>
> The room was about 40 feet long by 20 feet wide. Flowers were all around the casket and lined both sides of the room from floor to ceiling. The chairs were all empty. There was a large center aisle to the casket, and thick wall-to-wall red carpeting. As we approached the room, I noticed the silence. We crossed through the doorway and my daughter stopped and looked for a long time without saying a word — I waited. We approached the casket hand in hand. Grandma was laid out in a blue gown. My daughter looked at her for a long time and slowly turned, taking in the whole room again. Then she whispered, 'Mom, are we in heaven now?' "

The younger the child is, the more overwhelmed she may be at the enormity of the strange chapel. Viewing a drawing or diagram of the room ahead of time may be helpful. Also, if she can locate the funeral parlor on a map and see it in relation to her home, she may feel less threatened. Again, the most important advice regarding a child's attendance at funerals is that an adult whom she knows must be there to hold her hand. A child can derive comfort from the funeral only if she is physically secure.

It is important for a child to have tangible reminders of the deceased. Memorial stones help the child identify the exact spot where her parent is. Visits to the cemetery should not be discouraged.

Remember: the child has experienced the worst possible tragedy. She should feel terrible. If she is sent off to summer camp to forget and deny, she will not learn that she can, in fact, tolerate and overcome emotional catastrophes. Permitting the child to feel the loss when she is ready will increase her coping ability for the rest of her life.

4

BEREAVEMENT COUNSELING

Do you feel isolated?

Talking always helps. Words have the power to change attitudes and cure afflictions. The right words, from the right person, at the right time, can make a significant difference in your life.

When feelings are too powerful to be coped with, they are released from the body as physical or mental symptoms. Statistically, the bereaved are extremely susceptible to physical and emotional illness. However, those statistics are reversed when the bereaved can obtain emotional support from helpers who are aware of the psychological needs of mourners.

ROLE-MODELS

Surviving parents and children do best when they have the opportunity to discuss their predicaments with other families who have experienced a similar loss. In fact, all persons who experience the death of a loved one are helped by role-models, others who have survived the same ordeal. Role-models are living proof that one can survive such a trauma. You will find it easier to function when you can share your feelings with others who have experienced a similar loss. Parents of a deceased child wonder what to do with their child's room, toys and clothing. Parents who have been through it are best able to offer suggestions. Widows wonder about removing their wedding ring. Another widow is the best source of advice.

Children, in particular, welcome the opportunity to be amongst others of their age who have also lost a sister, brother or parent. They are relieved to find proof that while they may be the only one in their class or on their street who has had a death in the family, there *are* other youngsters who have lived through the same tragedy. Sharing a stigma relieves a burden and establishes a bond. Children do well in recreation groups where they can see other bereaved children now experiencing success in a sport or other activity. These children learn, from role-models, that sustaining a loss is just one part of being — not all of it. The role-models encourage them to develop the other parts of themselves.

BEREAVEMENT SUPPORT GROUPS

Bereavement groups, whose function is based on the philosophy that bereavement is a psychologically healthy and normal state, help mourners complete their grief work and get on with their lives. The aim of such groups is to facilitate the mourning process and prevent the serious effects of unresolved grief. The method is to offer mutual help through the support of a peer group. The group should meet weekly and focus on normalcy and health. Every group member becomes sensitive to another's feelings, hears the tears in another's voice, and begins to help by providing unselfish caring and sincere involvement. Alliances develop.

In the ideal community death would be dealt with openly. Every neighborhood or town would provide, along with schools and religious centers, a bereavement counseling service. Such a service would help facilitate the mourning process by providing groups that the bereaved could join. Each group would consist of a bereavement counselor and mourners belonging to a particular category — e.g.: parent groups for parents who have lost a child, widow groups, adult groups for adults who have lost a parent or other important person, exclusive of spouse or child, and two children's groups — one for children who have lost a parent and one for children who have lost a sibling. The bereavement counselor must be trained to recognize and appropriately respond to each stage of mourning.

A support group can provide the intimacy you need if you find that the current interaction you have with friends is inadequate. Particularly if you've lost the only person with whom you've ever experienced intimacy, a group will help you. Members of bereavement counseling groups tend to achieve intimacy quickly as they share emotions. While your neighbor may be so uncomfortable with her own thoughts about death and dying that when she sees you her impulse is to quickly cross the street, members of your group will have learned to acknowledge you and your feelings. They know you have some terrible feelings. They are prepared to hear you talk about those feelings.

Establishing and institutionalizing a ritual of attendance at a mutual-help group after a death in the family helps subvert the existing pressure to deny death inherent in our culture. Support groups are especially important to those whose loved ones who died from socially unacceptable causes, — such as suicide. If the circumstances of death cannot be spoken about, the bereaved gets no support. As you talk about your experiences and share your feelings with others you will become stronger. If you experience grief in isolation, you may lengthen the period of grief. If you need more help than a support group can give you, then six months to one year after the death, the time of intense second-stage mourning response, is usually the best time to seek professional intervention.

ANTICIPATORY GRIEF

An additional need is a group for those who are dealing with a fatal illness of a loved one. When death is imminent there is a process of anticipatory grief at work within the survivors. Did you begin to adjust to the idea of losing a beloved person *before* the actual death? This normal protective defense helps prepare you for the final reality of death. People need to share their experiences as they are going through anticipatory mourning so that a proper perspective is maintained.

OTHERS WHO CAN HELP

Your clergyman, or the rituals of your religion, may be of substantial help. Prayer permits intimacy without destroying needed defenses. Some clergymen have received special training in dealing with those in mourning, and may be of genuine help to the bereaved, both within and outside of their church.

It may surprise you to learn that many funeral directors have received special training in bereavement counseling. The media often classifies funeral directors as charlatans, and recent years have seen a general denigration of this industry by our society. Like every occupation, funeral directing has its unscrupulous few. Yet many in its profession continue to offer significant support and guidance to the family of the deceased with a dedication that goes ignored, or is misrepresented and misunderstood. Several years ago, at the Langley-Porter Institute in San Francisco, families of children who died of leukemia were asked to submit a list of those people who were most helpful to them in adjusting to their child's death. A majority of such grief-stricken parents indicated their funeral director as one of the important helpers in their time of need.

Think about this. According to studies, the average twenty year old young adult in our country has witnessed 12,000 homicides on TV but has never had any personal experience with death. Perhaps the funeral director has been stigmatized because he dares to deal with the realities of death and because his function does not permit the mourner to act as if the death is another TV fantasy.

Monument dealers, too, are sensitive to the needs of their bereaved customers. Memorial stones serve a necessary psychological function by providing a clear, tangible reminder of the deceased. The stone is often the focus of grief responses during the mourning period, and the focus of genealogical interest for subsequent generations when offspring investigate their heritage. Many bereaved individuals derive comfort from a simply designed memorial stone with a few meaningful words inscribed.

There *is* help for you. Unfortunately, if you do not live in an area with an outreach program for the bereaved, you may have to seek out the help by yourself. The important rules to remember are: (1) to avoid denying the situation; (2) admit that you will need some help in adjusting to your new circumstances; (3) locate the appropriate support system, and then; (4) learn to accept the support. Remember, mourning is a task which must be completed in order to get on with your life. You are entitled to all the help you can get.

5

insomnia

As you well know, after the loss of a loved one you experience many disturbing physiological symptoms of which sleeplessness is perhaps the most universal. The inability to get a full night's sleep prevents your body and your mind from replenishing themselves. Some people have difficulty falling asleep, others fall asleep rather easily but find themselves awakening many times, often every hour, throughout the night. Some mourners are plagued by early morning wakefulness—very early morning. These various forms of sleep disturbances are messages from your unconscious, warning that you need to speak about your thoughts and feelings. If insomnia persists for more than a few weeks please find a psychotherapist or bereavement counselor and arrange for some counseling sessions.

Below you will find some methods to help you regain your ability to experience normal sleep.

Please remember that if your sleeping difficulties are short-lived there will be no permanent damage to your health.

You may worry so much about not getting enough sleep that the worrying, not the lack of sleep, will cause you problems. Oh, you may feel tired or irritable, but you will not be ineffective at work or home. Normal performance at chores is usually not interfered with until you experience 3 consecutive nights of less than two hours sleep each night. There are no long-term effects of sleep deprivation. In experiments, persons deprived of all sleep for as long as 11 days were able to regain full emotional, physical, and intellectual abilities after 15 hours of sleep.

Most people do well with most of the methods described below. Remember that you are a distinct personality. Try each of these methods several times to discover the most suitable for you. No matter which method you use, you must first prepare your sleep environment to be free of distraction. Never stimulate yourself with coffee, tea, or cola in the evening. Those drinks contain caffeine which keeps your body awake and alert.

METHOD 1:

Lie still. Close your eyes, breathe deeply. Pretend you are asleep. Breathe as if you are asleep. This should put you to sleep in approximately 5 minutes.

METHOD 2:

As you lie in bed deliberately relax each part of your body. Begin with your toes. Feel each toe of each foot. Feel each ankle, then leg, then thigh. Now relax each finger. Continue up your arms until your shoulders feel loose. Next your back and buttocks. Your neck and head come last. When you relax your face concentrate on each area separately. Feel the muscles around your mouth and jaw become limp. Insist that your forehead be tension free—no frowning allowed. The process of entire body muscle relaxation takes about 15 minutes. Sleep will quickly follow.

METHOD 3:

Practice one of the following imagery exercises. Imagery is a mental picture obtained by closing your eyes and visualizing specific scenes. Which one of these (a, b, or c) imagery exercises most helps you sleep?

Scene (a):

You are a baby. You are sitting in your mother's lap. She is in a rocking chair. She holds you securely as she slowly rocks. She softly hums to the rhythm of the rocking chair. You drift off to sleep.

Scene (b):

You are taking a long walk. Your path winds through a tranquil countryside. Mountains are in the distance. A lake is below. You slowly walk through the grass. You see the mountains. You see the lake. You pause. You sit in a comfortable position. You hear the reassuring sounds of nature. You close your eyes. You are at peace with the world. You sleep.

Scene (c):

You are on a small private beach. You are coating yourself with mud. The mud is wet. Your body feels heavy from the weight of the mud. The mud is on your arms and legs. Now your chest and stomach are covered with mud, too. The mud weighs you down. You sink onto the sand. You are very heavy. You lie still, surrounded by wet sand, covered by cool mud. Your body is so heavy you cannot move. You cannot open your eyes. You sleep.

METHOD 4:

Establish bedtime rituals. Follow an exact routine every night beginning at least one half hour before you shut off your light. If your ritual includes food or drink be sure to have that same food or drink each night. If your ritual includes reading be sure to read from the same or similar book each night. Gradually your unconscious mind will associate your bedtime habits with sleep. Sleep will automatically follow your procedure!

METHOD 5:

Eat a food rich in tryptophane. Tryptophane is an amino acid which has natural sedative qualities. A steak dinner may make you feel tired because steak has tryptophane. Other such foods are milk (especially warm milk) and turkey. Have a tryptophane food as your last food in the evening.

METHOD 6:

Sometimes exercise will help you sleep. You should arrange to exercise both during the day and at bedtime. Exercise is any activity that exerts stress on a muscle. Dancing, participating in sports, walking, stairclimbing and toe-touching are examples of exercise activities. You and your physician should determine your unique exercise regimen. Many people find that an exercised body naturally seeks replenishment in sleep.

METHOD 7:

A warm bath will relax you. You may wish to add bubbles or bath oil to the tub. Luxuriate in the water. Pamper yourself. Feel the water rinse away your tension. The water should be comfortably warm, never hot. You will emerge from the tub feeling drowsy. Go directly to bed. You'll fall asleep promptly.

METHOD 8:

Specific sounds have a soothing effect upon your nervous system. A regular rhythm is monotonous and sleep inducing. You may choose a ticking clock, a rotating fan, or a vaporizor. Each will put you to sleep soon.

METHOD 9:

Count backwards. Begin with the number 500. Say each number to yourself. Picture the number in your mind. Slowly proceed to the next number. You will be sleeping before you reach zero.

METHOD 10:

Choose a dull book or newspaper article. Force yourself to read it. Do not skip any words. You need not understand what you are reading. Simply read.

The above methods will help you sleep soundly. Your sleep difficulties are appropriate during this time of bereavement. Soon your sleeplessness will be gone and you will once again enjoy relaxed, satisfying sleep.

6

SUICIDE

If someone in your family deliberately decided to die and systematically implemented a course of action that resulted in death, you are what is called a "survivor-victim" of suicide.

If you are a survivor-victim you are justifiably bewildered. You want to know what went wrong.

Usually there is no explanation.

Each year in the United States there are 25,000 reported suicides, and it is estimated that the actual number far exceeds 50,000. Families and physicians prefer to call a death accidental in order to guarantee life insurance payments to the survivors (standard life insurance policies exclude payment for death by suicide) and to avoid the stigma of suicide.

There are societies in which suicide is considered respectable and even morally obligatory. In our culture, however, suicide does have a negative value and that value often remains with the survivor-victims. Thus survivor-victims do not receive the social support that other mourners do receive. Neighbors and friends may avoid or even blame the family.

As a survivor-victim you may wonder what you could have done to prevent the suicide. You may feel perplexed and ashamed. You may feel isolated and alienated. You may feel angry. Ironically, the survivor-victim feels pain, while the suicide victim selected suicide to feel relief from pain.

Immediately after the suicide it is advisable to seek professional intervention. The initial shock, after learning of the catastrophic event, must be ameliorated. It is extremely important for each survivor-victim in the family to establish a therapeutic relationship with an experienced bereavement professional. Sometimes family members accuse one another or themselves of contributing to the act of suicide. The professional can help the family members understand their feelings and talk about their fears and fantasies. It is necessary for every family member to be told that they have free will and can choose not to follow the path of self-destruction.

Most of us choose to live. Even those of us whose circumstances may include illness, poverty, loneliness, and cruelty choose to live. Why, then, will some people choose death when their circumstances seem more fortunate?

The answer, of course, is that we cannot measure a person's inner torment, personal pain, or coping abilities. Suicide occurs when there is a permanent loss of hope. Suicide occurs regardless of social or economic status.

You may recall Edwin Arlington Robinson's poem about Richard Cory:

> Whenever Richard Cory went down town
>   We people on the pavement looked at him;
> He was a gentleman from sole to crown,
>   Clean favored, and imperially slim.
>
> And he was always quietly arrayed,
>   And he was always human when he talked;
> But still he fluttered pulses when he said,
>   "Good-morning," and he glittered when he walked.
>
> And he was rich—yes, richer than a king—
>   And admirably schooled in every grace:
> In fine, we thought that he was everything
>   To make us wish that we were in his place.
>
> So on we worked, and waited for the light,
>   And went without the meat, and cursed the bread:
> And Richard Cory, one calm summer night,
>   Went home and put a bullet through his head.

Most of us control our destructive impulses. We may overindulge in calories and/or cigarettes, but we stop short of total destruction. The suicide victim, however, was unable to develop and properly use coping mechanisms. The suicide victim was unable to deal with life's adversities and unable to deal with his or her inner life.

One person may tolerate a particular situation while another person may be driven to suicide by the identical circumstance. There is debate among mental health professionals regarding the mental status of suicidal people. Some psychologists believe that the act of suicide alone is sufficient evidence of mental illness, while others believe that a suicidal gesture may have no bearing on mental health. Suicide may simply be the final stage of continuous maladaptive behavior.

Please understand that life was unbearable for your loved one. There was too much pain. Life was simply beyond endurance. Death meant relief. Your loved one's suicide was beyond your control.

Senator Ted Kennedy spoke for all survivor-victims when he talked to the press upon the death of his 29-year-old nephew David Kennedy: "All of us loved him very much. With trust in God, we all pray that David has finally found the peace that he did not find in life."

7

letters

Mourners are sometimes comforted when they receive mail from a friend. Perhaps you, too, will feel comforted upon reading the letters reprinted below and the excerpt from a young girl's diary.

Dear Rose,

I just heard about your tragic loss, and I know that all the words in the world can't alleviate your pain.

When I lost my infant, I felt alone in my grief. My husband and family were disturbed and sad but only I was the mother, the one who carried the child for nine months. I was in charge of his well being. Was it my fault? Did I have a disease that I gave to the baby? I was filled with doubt. My beautiful baby died. Did I wish it the nights I was exhausted and confused by irregular sleep? NEVER! I spent months trying to go over how this tragedy might have been prevented. In time I reached a conclusion. I realized that there are no answers to some questions and we must do our best to go on with life.

This is why I am writing you this letter. First, I recommend crying and maybe even a little screaming; after all, you are hurting. I remember trying to be brave for all the people around me. I was wrong. If people really care for you they want to help. Use them, cry to them, tell them how you feel. Talk to your husband. He is hurting too. You both should hold each other up physically and mentally. People will say things they think will help, but hurt instead. The worst thing I heard was "You are young, you will have others." Stay away from people who unintentionally hurt you. People tend to forget that even though the baby lived for only a short time he was a person who died before his time. He had a right to life, and love. If you are like I was you feel a great personal injustice. Why me? Why him?

Step by step, day by day the pain gets duller. Like a deep wound it begins to heal; of course you have to use the right medicine. Which I found to be love, good friends, busy hands and positive thoughts about the future. I would think about the baby at certain times, I would cry and then I would go on with the things I had to do.

Rose, I still have my memories, The baby did exist and he was a part of me.

I hope this letter has encouraged you to go on and find that person inside you who will adjust and continue to survive in this best and worst of possible worlds.

If you need me call.

Love and Tears,

Carol

Dear Dorothy,

I have just returned home after attending your husband's funeral and your grief and sorrow were so overwhelming that I am reliving my own painful widowhood which began eight years ago. What I really wanted to do was reach out to you, embrace you and say "Everything will be alright," but instead I murmured the usual platitudes.

So now I must write you this letter. I don't even know if it will be a letter of condolence, but I think you will recognize so many of your own feelings that it will be of some comfort to know that your emotions are normal ones.

Like your Joe, my husband Philip was ill for so many years that my memories of him when he died were of his pain, his disability, and his courage. I had lived with fear of his dying for so long that I had guiltily imagined my life without him many times. In fact, I knew exactly how I would behave when he would die because 1) I was prepared, and 2) I was an intelligent, educated person. Right? Wrong—so wrong. I found out that no one is ever prepared for death and that grief has nothing to do with intelligence.

During my period of mourning I went through the gamut of emotions that tore away at my innards. Guilt, I think, was the strongest. Why hadn't I been kinder to him? Why hadn't I been a better sex partner? Why had I quarreled with him a week before his death? And so on and on I tortured myself. And then came the anger—how dared he leave me at a time in life when I needed him most! Next the regret. We had left so many things undone and so much unsaid. And of course, the self-pity was there all the time and the fear of facing life alone. I don't remember if I felt these one at a time or all at once, but it was self-torment at its most agonizing. I went through periods of time when I ate little or nothing, and at other times I gorged myself into oblivion.

Salvation came with my return to work. Aren't we lucky to be in a profession where we are with young people all the time? Dorothy, once I got back to school it was impossible for me to feel sorry for myself for too long. The youth, effervescence, excitement, and joy of life exuded by the kids was just what I needed.

Well, all of that is past history now. I have come to terms with my life and my aloneness. I take great pleasure and satisfaction in my children and grandchildren, although distance makes our meetings infrequent. After Philip's death I clung to the kids because they were part of him, but I soon realized that they must go their own way and I must go mine. For sheer survival, I have evolved a life style that is interesting and satisfactory. It took time, but I have made new friends, I travel, I enjoy many things I could not in the past. I often think of Philip wistfully and sentimentally and talk of our early life together to the grandchildren who love to hear those stories. It may sound like heresy, but I no longer miss him—I know he is at rest. I do, however, miss being married. I regret not having someone to share my life with, and someone for whom to care and to care for me.

On the other hand, after eight years of living alone I have become a very private person and I guard that privacy, and enjoy my own company. If I am not ecstatically happy (and who is?), neither am I unhappy. I find my days full and fruitful and have achieved a measure of contentment and serenity.

I have rambled on so that you will see a glimmer of light at the end of the dark tunnel. I know what you are feeling.

I am your friend during this sad time and always.

Love,

Hanna

Dear Mrs. Jackson,

This will not be an easy letter for me to write. It will bring back memories and cause some pain, but I'll write it, and go through a little heartache, with the hope that what I say will offer you some consolation and understanding.

I, too, lost a son from a drug overdose. He was my only child and 20 years old. He was tall, well built, and very handsome.

Unfortunately, he went through many tragedies in his young life. He was always sad. He rarely smiled.

The biggest tragedy of all was when his father died. He was 9 years old at the time but he understood what had happened.

From then on it was rough going for both of us. He loved his father very much and therefore rebelled against me and blamed me for his father's death. I did the best I could during that time. I know deep down in my heart I was a good mother.

It's 5 years since my son is gone, and I still remember very clearly the night it all happened.

After the shock of his death wore off, I was completely out of control. I couldn't cope with my normal every day routines. I went through the motions of life like a Robot—without feelings. I only did what I had to do. I began to hide from everyone and each day was torture for me. I began getting symptoms emotionally and physically that I didn't understand. It was then that I realized I needed professional help. I knew I couldn't go on the way I was.

After much tracking down, I finally got lucky and found a psychotherapist who specialized in Grief therapy. This was almost a year later. I began going for weekly sessions and they were sure rough. I left her office drained and emotionally exhausted.

After awhile, my symptoms began getting less and less and I was beginning to feel normal again. In time I gained control of myself and learned how to cope.

The pain is still there and always will be, but time does heal. I've finally accepted the fact that this is what my son wanted. Maybe he wanted to be with his father. I'll never know, but that is my only consolation even though I'm still hurt and angry at him for what he did.

I'm still in therapy but at least now I feel like the old me and can function again. My therapist saved my life. I get my good days and bad days but the difference now is, I don't panic during my bad days.

Only some one who has gone through the same tragedy can know what you're going through. I can talk about this now, but in the beginning, I couldn't. If any part of what I wrote will help comfort you, then it was worth my shedding tears today.

We'll always remember, and with a twinge of pain, but we have to go on for ourselves and others. "GOD" gives us the strength and time is a great healer. Good luck.

Sincerely,

Leonora

Dear Mike,

I know that to one who has just lost his mother, it is as if no one else knows how it feels.

Suddenly someone becomes ill, and we must anticipate loss. The throat lumps, the heart pounds and the fear of that separation becomes unimaginable. This cannot be happening to me, we think, in shock.

We grasp for meaning. We flash back over the movie reel that began with our first recollection. We fight desperately to remember, to have something to hold on to. We realize how distorted was our vision. Had we only known the treasure of the ordinary, simple details of life itself.

Nevertheless, tears flood our eyes as we face the unexplainable.

Now, sixteen years later, though my memory of my mother's illness is as vivid as if it were yesterday, I have come to a deeper understanding of the precious value of life. I try to look at a moment, not just with my eyes but with everything that is me.

Dearest friend, please believe that I understand the pain in your heart, the void in your gut, the cut-off feeling, the many things you never told her and the pain of knowing you never will. The agony of death, at this moment, for you is unbearable, but please, be patient. Time will soothe your pain.

With love and deep hopes that the time will pass quickly for you, I remain

Teri

Dear Mrs. Iranhower,

I am terribly sorry about what happened.

The same thing happened with my grandparents. Grandfather Gordon died. My mommy and daddy tell me don't worry grandma will be fine.

Don't worry Mrs. Iranhower, you'll miss him. Here's a poem for you.

> You'll miss Henry
> Yes you will
> You did all
> You could
> When he was ill

Love,

Martha I.

Dear Don,

I want to express my deepest sympathies at Janet's death. I think about her constantly. I am angry at the injustice of it all, at the insane, haphazard way in which tragedy strikes.

I'm trying to find answers, trying to attach blame, tending to withdraw into a self-protective cynicism. I know that I will have to find answers that I can live with, and that, perhaps, with my eventual, if reluctant, acceptance, I will find solace. I know that I will mourn her, pay homage in my thoughts, in my anger, in my sorrow and hopefully in my deeds. I know that I must acknowledge the depth of my feelings and not try to deny them.

How well and fondly do I cherish and remember the many wonderful hours spent with all of you at your home—with the baby crawling around, the girls in and out with their problems and comments, the pleasant cups of coffee we all enjoyed while chatting and working. Even though the memories are pouring in on me now, when I am feeling overwhelmed I try to escape. Perhaps it is better expressed in the following lines written by me (yes, I've taken to attempting to write poetry) which I call the "Buffer Zone." Maybe it will help you too.

THE BUFFER ZONE

I am enclosed in my buffer zone.
Nothing penetrates the batting,
   so insulated is this silence,
   lulling, its sound.

It permits of no distractions as
   the miles to the world lengthen,
   making remote its existence.

The din and pain are not allowed here.
It would absorb me into its depths
   as its waves envelop me.

With sealed eyes I surrender to its
   gentle vibrations.
Eager to be swallowed, I lie quietly
   listening to the muted sounds.

We merge, it and I, so hungrily do I
   drain it of its wealth.
It enters my total being, wrapping me
   in its protective invisible cocoon,
   washing its healing waters over me.

In time I will return renewed.

There is so much more I could say—about how she fought the cancer with her typical courage, about her great love for all of you, about how she would want you all to persevere, about the many bequests she left, but I'm sure you know all that and have heard it all many times. The only consolation to be had is the knowledge that she is now past all the pain and suffering. In time I know you will savor the wonderful memories you shared.

My best hopes for your future. Take care of yourselves and keep well.

Affectionately,

Sylvia

I am thirty three years old. My mother died of cancer when I was thirteen, and I thought the world had ended. I have learned that for me to understand death is to look closely and experience every feeling in life—love, hate, guilt, anger, sorrow, relief and even joy.

Here are some diary entries written during the week of my mother's death.

August 9,

Dear Diary,

Today was the most miserable and heart-aching day of my life. My mother has never been as sick as she was today. The whole world seemed strange to me. I cried every minute. Dear Diary, I want you to know that any little thing I can do for her, I'd do. I love her so much and my love and devotion for her will never die.

Love,

Teri

August 10,

Dear Diary,

I am trying to act like a grownup, but . . .

Love,

Teri

August 11,

Dear Diary,

Today is my dad's birthday!

August 13,

Dear Diary,

It happened. The most dreadful tragedy in a girl and her father's life. My mommie died yesterday. She fought terribly not to die on daddy's birthday and with her remarkable power, she didn't.

Today was the funeral. She looked just like a queen. I'm having a little girl someday and naming her Selma, the name I loved best.

Love,

Teri

Words can help you. They need not be sophisticated. They need only be sincere.

8

workshops for the widowed

Most women become widows.

In the United States today there are twelve million widowed persons, 85% of whom are women. Three out of four American women outlive their spouses. More than half of the women over 65 are widowed. The average age of American widows is 56. Only 7 of 100 widows 56 or older will remarry.

In some cultures mourning is expected to last for the remainder of the widow's life. It may not be pleasant, but at least the widow knows who she is and what is expected of her. She never has to give up her attachment to her dead husband. In our society, the official mourning period is of such short duration that it is usually over before the widow has a chance to understand what her new role in life is all about.

Widows should not expect to derive emotional support from their children. Even adult children may react to a parental death with all the irrationality of a small child. The widow's son or daughter may never before have lost a loved one or undergone an emotional crisis. Then, during adulthood, when a parental death occurs, it is the first confrontation with the "unfairness of life." Later, this person may find the remarriage of the widowed parent difficult to face. Adult children usually know that it is best for the surviving parent to love and be loved again. Yet their emotions may defy logic and they may become distressed at the thought of their parent's remarriage. As they come to terms with the fact that life is not always equitable, they begin to accept the parent's new mate. Even grown children, then, are often unable to offer their widowed parent a system of support.

Friends, family, clergymen and physicians all try to help the newly widowed. Logically they want her to recover as quickly as possible. It is usually only another widow who knows that grief must run its full course before it is possible to feel better again. The new widow has many things she needs to discuss — the circumstances of her husband's death, her fear of loneliness, her financial concerns, her feelings about the silent empty house — and the best partner for discussion is someone who has successfully negotiated these crises. Thus, another resource is the workshop for the widowed.

GETTING TOGETHER WITH OTHERS

Workshops for the widowed are planned events designed to help the widow gain strength and insight by providing a community of others who share similar predicaments. Such workshops have been successfully organized by community mental health centers, churches and synagogues, funeral homes and monument dealers, community colleges and senior citizen groups.

One characteristic of bereavement is difficulty in initiating new activity. Attending a scheduled workshop entails planning ahead, choosing an outfit to wear, arranging for transportation, and spending several hours in a social setting away from home. Making these decisions is a process that in itself is therapeutic.

The warm contact of a peer group which actively reaches out to the widow helps break her pattern of passivity. The workshop organizers must plan to contact the widow at the time she will be most likely to respond. The best time is after the first stage of mourning has been completed, when the kids have returned to their schools or separate homes, and the widow feels truly alone.

Social, cultural and economic boundaries are transcended by the universality of grief. As intimacies are exchanged among group members, caring relationships develop. Two workshop "graduates" recounted the following incident:

> *"Sara Jane, the petite widow of a prominent physician from Savannah, Georgia, was in a workshop with "Big Bertha," a janitor's widow who scrubbed office floors at night and cared for her seven children during the day. Shortly after the eighth workshop meeting, Sara Jane was wheeling her cart down the supermarket aisle when she heard a familiar voice. It was "Big Bertha" shopping for her brood. They were so delighted to see one another that each abandoned her cart and ran to embrace the other. Onlookers were puzzled by the incongruous pair. Sara Jane and Bertha simultaneously turned to explain, "We're almost family."*

Workshops may be organized in many ways. For example, the Widowed-to-Widowed Program developed by Dr. Phyllis Silverman at Harvard Medical School offers one-to-one counseling, with widows reaching out to other widows. The annotated bibliography that follows lists several sources which describe various workshop methodologies. All approaches have the objectives of helping the widow to understand and to accept her feelings, to become aware of the psychodynamics of the bereavement process, and to eventually re-enter life's mainstream.

Colleges, universities, social work and other community agencies are potential sources of information regarding grief counseling. Pick up the phone. Ask your religious leader or funeral director to help gather the data you need. The following chapter will help lead you to additional sources of information.

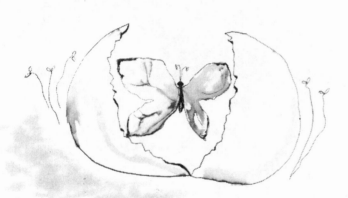

9

RESOURCE
materials

Thanatos was the mythological Greek God of death.

Thanatology is the study of death, dying, and bereavement. Contemporary society, as reflected in the media, has become fascinated with thanatology. Books, films, courses, and rap sessions dealing with death proliferate.

You may wish to formally study the subject as part of a high school or college continuing-education program. This opportunity is available in most cities today. In New York City, Brooklyn College offers a thanatology concentration within the department of Health Science, and New York University offers a summer institute in thanatology within the departments of Counselor Education and Religion Education.

Concern for Dying (250 West 57th Street, New York City, 10107) founded in 1967, is a non-profit, educational organization established to promote discussion of issues involved in death and dying. The Concern's primary goals are to create an environment that assures patient autonomy with regard to treatment during terminal illness, to prevent the futile prolongation of the dying process, and to eliminate the needless suffering of the dying.

Theoretical and philosophical investigations of matters pertaining to thanatology are explored in "packets" for sale from the Institute of Society Ethics and The Life Sciences (360 Broadway, Hastings-on-Hudson, New York 10706). Each packet contains articles reprinted from recent academic journals.

Christopher News Notes, available from The Christophers (12 East 48th Street, New York City, 10007) publishes occasional pamphlets dealing with death.

A hospice is an environment which is socially and psychologically beneficial to the terminally ill. You may contact the National Hospice Association (1311 Dolly Madison Blvd, McLean, Va. 22101) for further information. Also, Stephen and Ondrea Levine at The Dying Project (Box 2228, Taos, New Mexico 87571) may be of help.

The Foundation of Thanatology (630 West 168th Street, New York City, 10032) under the leadership of Dr. Austin Kutscher, offers several seminars and conferences each year.

"The Thanatology Library," an annotated catalog of all books and audio visual materials on thanatology, is available from The Center for Thanatology Research, a book service (P.O. Box 989, G.P.O. Brooklyn, New York 11201).

Lists of films on death and dying are available from The Educational Film Library Association (43 West 61st Street, New York City, 10023).

For help of a more personal nature you should know that many hospitals have outreach programs, (usually under the auspices of their social service departments) which offer counseling to the bereaved. Some community groups have established 24-hour telephone hot-lines and/or Widowed-to-Widowed programs.

The dying person may wish to contact a self-help organization called Make Today Count, (218 South 6th Street, Burlington, Iowa 52601) which holds weekly meetings for the dying at hundreds of locations throughout the United States.

The Widowed Persons Service, a program offered jointly by the National Retired Teacher's Association, The American Association for Retired Persons and Action for Independent Maturity (1909 K Street, N.W., Washington, D.C. 20049), is established in many United States cities and publishes a Directory of Services for the Widowed in the U.S. and Canada.

In specific geographic areas there are support organizations, such as Grief Groups, a bereavement counseling service (262 Coleridge Street, Brooklyn, N.Y. 11235); The Bar-Harris Center for Study of Separation and Loss (Chicago, IL.); The Center for Preventive Psychiatry (White Plains, N.Y.); Grief Education Institute (Littleton, Co); Center for Grief Counseling and Education (Madison, WI.); St. Francis Counseling Society (1768 Church Street, N.W., Washington, D.C. 20036).

The Society of Military Widows (P.O. Box 254, Coronado, California 92118) provides services for widows of veterans.

The American Association of Suicidologists (2459 S. Ash, Denver, Co. 80222, tel.# (303)692-0985) lists crisis intervention centers throughout the United States.

Compassionate Friends is a self-help organization for parents whose children have died. There are offices in almost all major cities. (Natl. Headquarters—P.O. Box 1347, Oak Brook, Ill. 60521)

Parents of Murdered Children provides help and mutual support throughout the United States. (Natl. Headquarters—1739 Bella Vista, Cincinnati, Ohio 45237)

SHARE is a national support group for parents who have lost an infant or who have experienced a miscarriage or stillbirth. (Natl. Headquarters—St. John's Hospital, 800 East Carpenter, Springfield, Ill. 62769)

The three organizations concerned with the problem of Sudden Infant Death Syndrome (SIDS) are: The National Clearinghouse for SIDS (Suite 600, 1555 Wilson Boulevard, Rosslyn, Va. 22209); The National SIDS Foundation (Two Metro Plaza, Suite 205, 8240 Professional Place, Landover, MD. 20785); and National Headquarters—Council of Guilds for Infant Survival (P.O. Box 3841, Davenport, Iowa 52808).

The Theos Foundation (306 Penn Hills Mall, Pittsburgh, Pa. 15235) is a Christian fellowship for widows. Also in this category are the NAIM Conference (Chicago, IL) and the Post CANA Conference (Washington, D.C.).

The Monument Industry Information Bureau (MIIB) is an international organization created to provide information to the public on memorialization. Booklets and other written material can be obtained through MIIB by writing to the Bureau at 444 N. Michigan Avenue, Suite 1600, Chicago, Illinois 60611.

When seeking help in your community, don't overlook the clergy. Most clergymen will try to meet your needs, whether or not you are a congregation member.

Good luck to you in your search for solace.

CONCLUSION

Philosopher, Arnold Toynbee, in his essay "Reflections on My Own Death," has stated that true love might be proved by the wish of a person to outlive his loved one, so that the loved one is spared the anguish of grief.

Rich or poor, young or old, no one is exempt from the devastating effects of grief. All mourn. All suffer.

Everyone who lives a full life must, at some time or another, live with an empty chair. Whether the chair you live with belonged to a parent or spouse, a child or lover, a best friend or relative, it is empty now, and its emptiness represents a task for you. To accomplish this task is to become accustomed to living with that empty chair. When you no longer fear it or revere it, but can simply accept it, you will know that you are completing your grief work.

RECOMMENDED READING

These books and articles have been
found to be helpful by lay people and
professionals alike.

All titles listed are available from
The Center For Thanatology Research & Education,
391 Atlantic Ave., Brooklyn, N.Y. 11217.

CHAPTER 1

Becker, E. *The Denial of Death*. New York: The Free Press, 1973.
> (A Pulitzer Prize winner, this book approaches death with the tools of a cultural anthropologist.)

Feifel, H. (ed.) *New Meanings of Death*. New York: McGraw-Hill, 1977.
> (A collection of important essays and articles concerning death.)

Grollman, E.A. *Concerning Death: A practical Guide For the Living*. Boston: Beacon Press, 1974.
> (Medical, religious, legal, and psychological questions about death are answered with quiet reassurance and good advice.)

Kubler-Ross, E. *On Death and Dying*. New York: Macmillan Co., 1969.
> (A Classic—shows concern and compassion for the dying patient and attempts to organize the psychological stages of death.)

Kubler-Ross, E. *Questions and Answers on Death and Dying*. New York: Macmillan Co., 1974.

Kubler-Ross, E. with Mel Warshaw. *To Live Until We Say Goodbye*. New York: Prentice-Hall Inc., 1978.
> (A sensitive photo-essay of Dr. Ross' adult and children patients who speak candidly about their terminal illnesses.)

CHAPTER 2

Bowlby, J. *Attachment and Loss*. New York: Basic Books, Inc. Vol. I - *Attachment*, 1969; Vol. II - *Separation*, 1973; Vol. III - *Loss*, 1980.
> (Dr. Bowlby indicates that early experiences of separation determine future reactions to loss.)

Bowlby J. "Grief and Mourning in Infancy and Early Childhood." *The Psychoanalytic Study of the Child*, Vol. 15 (1960).

Bowlby, J. "Processes of Mourning." *International Journal of Psychoanalysis*, Vol. 42 (1961) pp. 317-340
> (Bowlby's studies are classics in determining the importance of consistent mothering during infancy. He defines the beginning of the mourning process as a search for a reunion with the deceased, the middle of the process as an angry rage and the end of mourning as a detachment from the deceased.)

Carr, A. et al. (eds.) *Grief: Selected Readings*. New York: Health Sciences Publications Corp., 1975.
> (Excellent compilation of studies, essays, and discussions.)

Clayton, Desmarais, and Winokur. "A Study of Normal Bereavement." *The American Journal of Psychiatry*, Vol. 125 (1968).
> (Depressed mood, sleep disturbance and weeping seem to be the common bereavement symptoms.)

Darwin, C. *The Expression of the Emotions in Man and Animals*. London: Murray, 1872.
> (Animals grieve, too!)

Deutsch, H. "The Absence of Grief." *The Psychoanalytic Quarterly*, Vol. 6 (1937).
> (Studies of children, and some adults, who adopt an attitude of indifference in order to protect their egos from feeling the pain of grief.)

Freud, S., J. Strachey (ed.) *The Standard Edition of the Complete Psychological Works of Sigmund Freud*. London: Hogarth, 1957. "The Ego and the Id" Vol. 19 (1923).
"Inhibition, Symptoms and Anxieties" Vol. 20 (1926).
"Mourning and Melancholia" Vol. 14 (1917).
> (Powerful reading—particularly "Mourning and Melancholia," which describes how repressed ambivalence toward the deceased can cause pathological mourning.)

Gorer, G. Death, Grief and Mourning. Garden City, New York: Doubleday, 1967.
> (Emphasizes the need for a secular mourning ritual.)

Lindemann, E. "Symptomatology and Management of Acute Grief." *American Journal of Psychiatry,* Vol. 101 (1944) pp. 141-148.
(A classic study of the families of the victims of the Cocoanut Grove Fire, 1942.)

Parkes, C. *Bereavement: Studies of Grief in Adult Life.* New York: International Universities Press, 1972.
(Case histories.)

Parkes, C. "The First Year of Bereavement." *Psychiatry,* Vol. 33 (1970) p. 444.

Schoenberg, B. et al. *Bereavement: Its Psychosocial Aspects.* New York: Columbia University Press, 1975.
(A compilation of thirty-one scholarly works about bereavement and the role of the professional.)

Schoenberg, B., Carr, A., et al. *Loss and Grief.* New York: Columbia University Press, 1970.
(Psychological management of the patient and the patient's family.)

CHAPTER 3

Cook, S. *Children and Dying: An Exploration and Selected Bibliographies.* New York: Health Sciences Publishing Corp., 1974.

Fassler, J. *My Grandpa Died Today.* New York: Human Sciences Press, 1971.
(Written for young children.)

Furman, E. *A Child's Parent Dies.* New Haven: Yale University Press, 1974.
(Research tracing the lives of children, through adulthood, after a parental death.)

Green, P. *A New Mother for Martha.* New York: Human Sciences Press, 1978.
(A picture book for first through third graders.)

Grollman, E. (ed.) *Explaining Death to Children.* Boston: Beacon Press, 1967.
(Expert advice to parents.)

Grollman, E. *Talking About Death: A Dialogue Between Parent and Child.* Boston: Beacon Press, 1971, 2nd edition 1975.
(Excellent for young children.)

Krementz, J. *How It Feels When A Parent Dies.* New York: A. Knopf, 1982.
(Sensitive photos, truth.)

Le Shan, E. *Learning to Say Good-Bye.* New York: Macmillan Publishing Co. Inc., 1976.
(Sensitive book for children.)

Miller, J. "Children's Reactions to the Death of a Parent: A Review of the Psychoanalytic Literature." *Journal of the American Psychoanalytic Association,* Vol. 19 (1971), pp. 697-719

Nierenberg, H.A. and Fischer, A. *Pet Loss.* New York: Harper and Row, 1982.
(A thoughtful guide for parents and children.)

Temes, R. *The Empty Place.* New York: Irvington Publishers, 1984.
(A boy adjusts to the death of his sister.)

Wolfenstein, M. "How is Mourning Possible?" *The Psychoanalytic Study of the Child,* Vol. 21 (1966), pp. 93-123.

CHAPTER 4

Bailey, L. R. *Biblical Perspectives on Death*, Philadelphia: Fortress Press, 1979.
(A rendering of every statement made about death in the Old and New Testament with historical commentary.)

Donnelly, K.F. *Recovering From the Loss of a Child*. New York: Macmillan, 1982.
(The best book, yet, for bereaved parents. Indispensable, excellent directory of local helping organizations.)

Gunther, J. *Death Be Not Proud*. New York: Harper and Row, 1971.
(Parents' account of their son's terminal illness.)

Greenberg, S. *A Treasury of Comfort*. Hartford, Conn.: Hartmore House, 1954.
(A compilation of helpful readings selected mostly from the Bible and the major poets.)

Hajal, F. "Post-Suicide Grief Work in Family Therapy." *Journal of Marriage and Family Counseling*, April 1977.

Kutscher, A. and L. *For the Bereaved*. New York: Frederick Fell, Inc., 1971.
(Excellent selections from literature, the Bible, etc.)

Moffat, Mary Jane. *In the Midst of Winter*, New York: A.E. Knopf, 1982.
(An anthology of consolation messages from aching friends to the grief stricken, drawn from literature of the ancient Romans to the present.)

Wechsler, J. *In A Darkness*. New York: Irvington Publishers, 1983.
(A father's truthful and poignant account of his son's mental illness and death.)

CHAPTER 5

Gnap, John J. M.D. *Easy Sleep.* Briarcliff Manor, N.Y.: Stein and Day, 1978.
> (A book meant for those with sleeping problems. Author provides step by step formula for overcoming chronic insomnia and occasional sleep difficulties using relaxation and concentration exercises: how to take control of your sleeping habits and make them work for, rather than against, you.)

Kellerman, Henry, Ph.D. *Sleep Disorders: Insomnia and Narcolepsy.* New York: Brunner/Mazel, 1981.
> (Reference book on insomnia (the inability to sleep) and narcolepsy (the compelling need to sleep). Book written for physicians, mental health workers, and students. Relates personality factors to biological aspects of sleep. A study of the various theories of sleep disorder, diagnosis and treatment.

Pai, M.N. *Sleeping Without Pills.* New York: Stein & Day, 1966.
> (A short book, easy to read; meant for those with chronic insomnia and occasional sleep problems. Author discusses the physiology and psychology of sleep and gives advice based on clinical experience.)

Regestein, Quentin R., M.D. *Sound Sleep.* New York: Simon & Schuster, 1980.
> (The author explains to the reader how to understand the nature of sleep problems, how to trace them to understand the nature of sleep problems, now to trace them to underlying causes, and how to correct them. Book is organized into a self-use system that can be used at home. Regestein is the director of the Sleep Clinic at Harvard's Peter Bent Brigham Hospital. The book also includes a listing of where to find professional help and how to take full advantage of it.)

Schwartz, Alice Kuhn, Ph.D. *Somniquest: The Five Types of Sleeplessness and How to Overcome Them.* New York: Harmony Books, 1979.
> (Five types of insomnia defined, isolated, and described. A chapter is devoted to each and illustrated with case histories. Author explains how to combat sleep difficulties with a combination of food and exercise. Also includes list of sleep clinics.)

Williams, Robert L. M.D. and Karacan, Ismet, M.D. (MED), D.Sc. *Sleep Disorders, Diagnosis and Treatment.* New York: John Wiley & Sons, 1978.
> (Primary and secondary sleep disorders are studied and treatment steps are provided for the clinician.)

Usdin, Gene, M.D. *Sleep Research and Clinical Practice.* New York: Brunner/Mazel, 1973.
> (A short, concise book to help the clinician. Includes chapters by sleep pioneer William C. Dement, who reviews the current neurochemistry of sleep. Provides basic, technical information explaining the meaning and derivation of terms and common uses. Also includes a chapter by Robert Williams and Ismet Karacan, who provide a complete listing of sleep disorders. A chapter by Anthony and Joyce Kales illustrates how sleep studies can help clinicians in diagnosing and treating patients.)

Moore-Ede, Martin, et al. *The Clocks that Time Us: Physiology of the Circadian Timing System.* Harvard University Press, Cambridge, Mass., 1982.
> (An excellent text for the student, professional, and layman which explains the new discipline of circadian rhythms including the effects of sleeping pills, jet lag, etc.)

CHAPTER 6

Dublin, Louis I., Ph.D *Suicide: A Sociological and Statistical Study.* New York: Ronald Press, 1963. (Includes case histories, an examination of the prevalence of suicide in our society, historical background and a study of suicidal motives and means of prevention. Recommended for the professional as well as the lay reader.)

Durkheim, Emile. *Suicide, A Study in Sociology.* Glencoe, Ill.: Free Press, 1951. (Originally published in 1897.) (A classic in suicidology. Durkheim believes that suicide, which appears to relate solely to the individual and his or her particular situation, is really a social problem and can be logically explained by the social structure. Explains in detail the three categories of suicide: egoistic, altruistic and anomic. An important text meant for those intending to study the subject in great detail.)

Hendin, Herbert, M.D. *Suicide in America.* New York: W.W. Norton & Company, 1982. (The complete up-to-date book on suicide; fast, easy reading. Answers all questions relating to suicide in the U.S.: Who commits suicide and why; the methods of suicide and what they mean; suicide and psychotherapy; social policy towards suicide.)

Klagsbrun, Francine. *Too Young to Die.* Boston: Houghton Mifflin Co., 1976. (Suicide among young people. Easy to read. The author does not delve into technicalities, but discusses the problem of young suicide through case studies and examples. Findings based on surveys, interviews. Intended for young adults, parents and teachers.)

Mack, John E. *Vivienne, The Life and Suicide of an Adolescent Girl.* Boston: Little Brown & Co., 1981. (Fourteen-year-old Vivienne Loomis committed suicide by hanging herself. She left behind a diary and other papers and letters which the authors piece together to understand the reason for her death. Part I of the book contains Vivienne's papers and the story of her life. In part II the author applies the reason for her death to adolescent suicide in general. Interesting reading for all those interested in the subject.)

Maris, Ronald W. *Pathways to Suicide, A Survey of Self Destructive Behavior.* Baltimore, Md.: The Johns Hopkins University Press, 1981. (A data-based theory of suicide, using sophisticated statistical tools and procedures. Explores social and psychological dynamics of suicide. The book is highly readable giving reasons, explanations and a carefully drawn out conclusion. Meant more for suicide investigators, but understandable by all.)

Neuringer, Charles and Lettieri, Dan J. *Suicidal Women: Their Thinking & Feeling Patterns*. New York: Gardner Press, Inc., 1982.

(Authors feel it is a subject largely ignored, and therefore have put together this short but complete book examining the nature of suicide in general and the suicidal behavioral patterns of women in particular. Relatively easy to read; short and direct, well organized under headings and subheadings.)

Prentice, Ann E. *Suicide: A Selective Bibliography*. Metuchen, N.J.: The Scarecrow Press, Inc., 1974.

(A selection of more than 2000 books and articles, for the needs of the general researcher.)

Colt, G.H. "Suicide in America," *Harvard Magazine*. Sept/Oct, 1983.

(Why the suicide rate continues to rise despite the existence of more than 300 prevention centers throughout the country. Writer draws on a number of theories by various experts in the field. Good reading; well researched.)

"Why 30,000 Americans Will Commit Suicide This Year," *U.S. News & World Report*. April 2, 1984.

(Interview with author and suicidologist Ronald Maris, who theorizes that family-life disarray, job competition and the decline in religious values contribute to a feeling of hopelessness that leads to suicide.)

CHAPTER 8

Eberhardt, L. *A Woman's Journal.* Columbia, Maryland: New Community Press, 1976.
>(A book of consciousness-raising and self-discovery exercises for women. Widows who complete a successful widow workshop often wish to continue meeting together as a self-awareness group.)

Glick, I.O., Weiss, R.S. and Parkes, M.C. *The First Year of Bereavement.* New York: John Wiley & Sons, 1974.
>(Offers Dr. Parkes' pioneering research about widows.)

O'Neill, G. and N. *Shifting Gears.* New York: Avon Books, 1974.
>(Guidelines for creating growth from conflict.)

Reuben, D. *Any Woman Can!* New York: Bantam Books, 1971.
>(An especially helpful chapter on sex, men and widows.)

Seskin, J. *Young Widow.* New York: Ace Books, 1975.
>(A newlywed describes her husband's terminal illness.)

Sheehy, G. *Pathfinders.* New York: William Morrow & Co., Inc. 1981.
>(Pathfinders are people who successfully negotiate the normal, predictable crises of living. This is an inspiring book.)

Simon, S. et al. *Values Clarification.* New York: Hart Publishing Co., 1972.
>(Exercises to help determine personal value systems are often appropriate after the loss of a crucial person.)

Silverman, P. et al. *Helping Each Other in Widowhood.* New York: Health Sciences Publishing Corp., 1974.
>(Experiences of the founders of the Widow-to-Widow outreach program.)

Silverman, P. *If You Will Lift the Load.* Hackensack, New Jersey: Jewish Funeral Directors of America, 1976.
>(Methods of establishing mutual-help groups.)

Strugnell, C. *Adjustment of Widowhood and some Related Problems.* New York: Health Sciences Publishing Corp., 1974.
>(A comprehensive annotated bibliography.)

Two booklets of particular interest to widows are: "Your Retirement Widowhood Guide" and "On Being Alone." Both are available from: American Association of Retired Persons, 1909 K Street, N.W., Washington, D.C. 20049.

CHAPTER 9

Adler, et al. *We are But a Moment's Sunlight.* New York: Pocket Books, 1976.
(Plentiful collection of interesting literary excerpts concerning death and bereavement.)

Mills, G. et al. *Discussing Death.* Homewood, Illinois: ETC Publications, 1976.
(A guide for teachers of death education from kindergarten through high school.)

Schneidman, E. *Death: Current Perspectives.* Palo Alto, California: Mayfield Publishing Co., 1976.
(Collection of academic papers concerning all aspects of death.)

Schneidman, E. "Death Questionnaire" *Psychology Today,* Vol. IV, #3, (August 1970) Del Mar, California: C.R.M., Inc.